Baby's First Apocalypse

Poems By Zara Lisbon

Luchador Press
Big Tuna, TX

Copyright © Zara Lisbon, 2021
First Edition: 1 3 5 7 9 10 8 6 4 2
ISBN: 978-1-952411-56-4
LCCN: 2021932859

Cover image and author photo: Scott Antonucci, Omar Doom
All rights reserved. No part of this publication may be
reproduced or transmitted in any form or by any means,
electronic or mechanical, including photocopying,
recording or by info retrieval system, without prior
written permission from the author.

Acknowledgments:

First of all, I want to thank my parents, Caron and Mark, for encouraging me to write poetry from the time I first showed interest at eight or nine years old.

I'm so grateful to everyone who has supported my poetry writing over the years: Scott Antonucci, Jenny Rae Bailey, Mathieu Cailler, Hannah Denyer, Mathew Dickman, Quinn Falconer, Mira Gonzalez, Brad Kaiserman, Natasha Lipson, Sarah Maclay, Ariel Morris, and Robert Wieder.

This book would not be possible without the inspiration of Leonard Cohen, E.E Cummings, Lana Del Rey, Stephen Dunn, T.S Eliot, Lawrence Ferlinghetti, Jack Kerouac, David Lynch, Jamaal May, Joni Mitchell, Pablo Neruda, Conor Oberst, Morgan Parker, Sylvia Plath, Mathias Svalina, and, undeniably, Taylor Swift.

Lastly, I must acknowledge my grandmothers Ellie and Doreen, who have been shining lights during my darkest times.

The poem "Nobody Lives Here" was published in *FORTH magazine* in 2014

TABLE OF CONTENTS

Core / 1

There are two types of people who don't eat / 2

News these days / 3

Virgin America / 5

Girls of the Pacific Northwest / 8

How To Become a Swiftie / 12

Yoyo / 20

Strange Pleasures Part 1 / 21

Praying for Syria / 22

Watch the Rain / 26

Photographs From a Disposable Camera / 27

Another Fucking Taylor Swift Poem / 36

Nobody Lives Here / 37

Oxy-codeine moon-light of a window-rippled street-lamp / 39

Dislocation 1 / 41

Dislocation 2 / 42

Midnight and Always / 44

Misha / 45

Thoughts in Vermont / 47

The Drive Home from Moonshadows / 48

X-BOX / 50

Hint / 53

Red Vines / 54

Strange Pleasures Part 2 / 56

What You Did / 57

Very Rich / 59

You Said You Would / 60

In Case You're Wondering / 62

Carpe Noctum / 63

Strange Pleasures Part 3 / 64

Degrees of Sparkle / 65

Sorry / 69

Madison Avenue / 70

Selfish / 71

First Love / 75

Pen to Paper / 76

Diet Coke / 79

Strange Pleasures Part 4 / 80

Apocalypse Currently / 81

Toxic / 82

Walking Home Alone in a Pandemic / 85

I Could Sleep Forever / 87

To Scott and Shiloh

The end approaches, but the apocalypse is long lived.

-Jacques Derrida

Core

Should I get drunk and put together a poem
about how much I hate the word poetry
and its inability to cover ground?

I will drink to feel clean and tell you
about how I am made up of these metal pieces
fused together at the joints, covered in satin, and how
this makes me feel
ridiculous.

Ridiculous and exposed and curious about myself
for the first time, like it's only just now occurring to me
that I have been alive
all along. A marionette created in the imagination
of a megalomaniac genius,
but alive.

I've been thinking of buying a stripper pole for my room
just so I can try to find my core.

And then what? I will find it and open the little metal door
that leads
to the center of me
and find that it's only magnets. Magnets and light.

I've been thinking about you
and magnets and how one sentence doesn't need to relate
to the next in order for it to count as a poem. How one
sentence doesn't need to relate to the next in order for it to
count as a conversation:

There are two types of people who don't eat

There are two types of people
Who don't eat:
1) Those who eat kale, drink soup
and collagen juice
2) Those who eat m&ms and
Honey Bunches of Oats in a cup
and that's it.
I am the latter.
Not that I'm anorexic,
necessarily—actually my mom says I look healthy lately—
I'm just preoccupied.
I just like fucking with a sense of control:
winning it then losing it
then winning it back again.

I have more to say than just that.
I have lines in my mind
running all day long but when
I pick up a pen
they're gone.
They're phobic of ink
and existing on paper
the way I am phobic of spiders
and their too many eyes
and the concept of holes
that hold an infinity of secrets
that I could fall into
and never escape.

News these days

No news is good news.
Meaning, if you don't receive any news, it can only mean
that all is good.
But also,
no news is good news
meaning, there is no news you could ever receive
that could possibly be good.

Two billion years ago up to 99% of life on earth died.
Are we due for another extinction?
Maybe,
but what really kills me
is that I can't write a song about it.
Leave the magic to the songwriters, I tell myself
but there's an empty notebook on the shelf
that wants to be held
the way a baby wants to be held
with arms outstretched
and it wants blood
the way a vampire does
selfish and helplessly.

It wants the stories of bruises I've worshipped
and bruises I've lost sleep over
driving west on Santa Monica Boulevard
with the owls in the middle of the night
—their good-time drinks and their feel-good vibes—
when I am nothing but cursed.

Cruel and jealous and cursed for my sins
which, at this point, are numerous.
Don't laugh, just take my fucking word for it.
Just take me back to Mount Olympus
where we listened to Lana Del Rey in the dark
drank Pepsi cola from a can
to feel real cute.
I'd put the nostalgia of you in my veins any day.

The feeling that I am inadequate
is just so dramatic.
It never gets easier,
I just find more people who I'm not.
It's just a feeling, but it's one that I can't shake.
It's just in my head
but, as Marianne Williamson says,
that's the most dangerous place.

This still isn't a song and I hate that.
I will get to heaven and still live to please.
I will be in heaven still wanting to please you all.
I will get down and crawl
on hands and knees
until you are people pleased.

Virgin America

LAX is nobody's home
pine-scented antiseptic glossed across linoleum-igloo floors
glittering like a thousand demons under fluorescent light
reflecting the waxy dread of "nothing."
The triplet girls at gate 25A in velvet and pigtails are too young to know
their tedious fate to be brought on
by this placeless place.

It is the necromancy of disappearing from place to place
that eviscerates any sense of home
and every sun-kissed, moon-bent sliver I have known
erased in the face of a blue- carpet floor
suspended above thirty-thousand miles of nothing
with plastic plates of elephant-skin grey to shield the light

of an ever-nearing sun.
And slowly swiveling bulbs of lilac light grow
like onions from the ceiling: planet convex and rattling—
I know this trembling is standard, even dull, and there is
nothing to get existential about, but the cranberry panic
tastes like home,
coasts like silicone along the roof of my mouth and the floor
of my chest. Look around: polyester reds and tubular ice
cubes: this is the place
where you will die. Or at least one crucial part. You know,

Death is not an end or a fate, but a practice—
a slipping towards light
that evades us like
floating dust illuminated by golden rays
that cascade onto the floor.
I rise, I rise: Xanax snowflakes dissolve warm and bright into
my mind. Never a place so warm and so bright.
When somebody whispers: *There's no place like home*
it sounds like a stranger's hands, cold against my flesh.
Meaning nothing.

Sometimes the only remedy is desire, but it is
those times that nothing excites me.
There is nothing here to touch, to welcome, to know.
Below, beige and indigo intertwine like vessels beaten to
abstraction around the homes of the grounded.
I order whisky: it tastes like light.
But what do you know of this place?
Call it Nightmare, if you will. With crystalline ceilings and
maggots in the floorboards.

We've been unfaithful as this ceiling is to the floor:
converging with clouds: It can be mathematically proven
that my nothing comes from your nothing.
Maybe I resent you adopting me out to this place.
You wrote: *A thing doesn't exist if it can't be known*
to intellect, that is quietly divine and holier than the taste of
fresh light.
Follow it high and higher, it will lead you home.

Instead, I will descend into a ringed and burning home of fiery floors. Oh, blinding light, Oh blissful nothing:
open holes in my deceptive knowledge and I will forever belong to your darkest place.

Girls of the Pacific Northwest
(A tribute to Laura Palmer of Twin Peaks)

I saw my blood   deep
crimson blue
laid out for me in seven test tubes

like
maraschino and grenadine

on
cocktail night
like

the lips of whores I've wanted to be.

I saw you   staring
hollow-
eyed
from across   the room
bent and brooding   in the pain of daylight—

Your skin   frosted over   as a mausoleum,
your mouth   a succulent fruit   broken open.

You were conditioned
to stillness:
The stillness became you, and you became
its loyal servant:

an
owl
caught
in
a
ring
of
trees.

I triggered something in you.
I didn't mean
to pull that trigger. I didn't mean
to turn you on.

Or to turn on you.

But it was too easy: all it took was being
human.

                                  All it took was
being

pure.

The purest of the pure,   through your eyes.

You didn't know
the sins
I collect like   pearls:

Your teeth

were not the first to   venture

beneath my flesh.

You were not the first to drink me colorless.

Like a burning, flickering beacon   I attract the

darkness—

it has fed on me since I
was
twelve

entering
through my open window, each night
disguised as a derelict lover

covered
        in ash,
                missing
                        teeth.

He took my

smile   for his collection
of polished trinkets—

blackened my lips,
yellowed my teeth.

Then all I was			was solid twilight.

Then all I could do
was wait

for death disguised
as a suburban father		to take me away from myself.

I saw my blood,
deep crimson blue		splattered across the rusted

walls of
an abandoned train.

And you were there with
my smile			in your hands

Ready to wrap me up in plastic.

How To Become a Swiftie

Fall 2008
Love Story

You're eighteen and home from art school
for a week because
your anxiety has become an absurdist work of art.

You can't stop visualizing catastrophe,
the very worst-case scenario
around every corner. Bombs on airplanes, your boyfriend
at the time
falling off the face of the anime-sketched earth
with other girls
becoming two-dimensional,
irretrievable. *I talked to your dad
go pick out a white dress* seems kinda sexist but
you'll take it.
You listen on repeat
and keep it
a secret.

Summer 2012
We Are Never Ever Getting Back Together

You turn it off halfway through
because your ex has someone new
and you

can't believe it's really over. You can't believe you're
never…you're actually really probably this time never,
ever, ever…
and this poppy anthem-to-be cuts you wherever it touches
so you avoid it at all costs
drinking obscure gin beverages on your lunch breaks
at Musso and Franks.
You don't talk to your friends or talk to his friends. And
nobody talks
to you.

Summer 2014

Blank Space

Think: this sounds like new Taylor Swift and *wow
girl knows how to write a song* and *what is
'get along with Starbucks lovers?'*
Since your breakup in 2012 you've added three names
to your short list of ex-lovers
and you wonder
what it would really be like to date Taylor Swift, and you
wonder
what it would be like to spill your soul for the entire world
tell the truth
name names
and get paid. You wonder what Taylor's parents think
when she tells the world about her long list of ex-lovers
and what your parents would think
if you told the world
about yours. Then wonder why you care.

Taylor doesn't.
Opinions are water off her velvety back.

Spring 2016
Famous by Kanye West

On the Pacific Coast Highway driving south
You say out loud
OH MY GOD,
WHAT? and know
shit is about to go down. You know
it's the end of an era. You know
you'll always remember where you were—the ocean glistening
like a hot metal grill—when you first heard Kanye say:
I made that bitch famous.

Summer 2017
Look What You Made Me Do

The single has dropped but
you're too tied up to listen.
Literally.
You've let this girl you wish you hadn't met
bind your wrists above your head and
it's one of those very temporary bedrooms where
the mattress is on the floor
and the dresser is made of plastic
and the TV is a computer covered in glitter and stickers.
She smokes and makes you watch some TV show from
Poland that is funny if you understand Polish humor.

You don't.
In the morning you drive away FAST
listening to *Look What You Made Me Do* LOUD, your bones
and teeth feeling like loose change clanging and clattering
around, threatening to roll free and the old era, the old
world, the way things used to be
can't come to the phone right now
or ever again.

April 2019

it is uncomfortable waiting with the masses, feeling
like a sheep, watching the clock countdown until
God knows what.
You want to say:
YOUR SOLAR FLARES ARE FAKE, YOUR PASTELS ARE
MANIPULATIVE, but
there's a too-sweet pulse thwacking in your veins, pooling
in your gut telling you
it's all as real
and as genuine
as the moment you wake up in the morning
and know that one of these days it'll be for the last time.

4.26
Me!

All day you're thinking about me.
Not the me that is you, but the me
that is Taylor Swift. The real me. Owning a decadent

collection of flaws
and calling them gems. Asking
for the spotlight and wearing it comfortably
like a second skin.
That *me* is buried somewhere under backlot cobblestone pastel
and years of shedding snakeskin
turned to butterflies
turned to dust.

At the stroke of Midnight Eastern
you sneak away in search of reception and find it outside
in the Los Angeles concept of cold
by a congregation of valet-parked Maserati's
packed in tight, perched and silken
like a murder of crows. You hold the phone to your ear
and you shiver as you listen for the First Time thinking
where, God, please tell me where, does this confidence come from?
And how does one find a place in this world among
the warring colors of a rainbow and the
non-stop
nonchalance
of all the cool chicks out there?
You think why is Taylor Swift 29 and still fighting in the rain?
which really means:
Why have I never fought in the rain? Why have I never kissed
in the rain?
A flower doesn't compare itself
To the flower standing next to it, it just grows.
What a lovely sentiment, you say to nobody, but
Do I look like a fucking flower to you?

You go home and watch the Music Video
on repeat, looking for a sign
That Taylor Swift is the all-knowing,
the unmoved mover, the puppet master who pulled
the strings of these cosmos together once upon a time,
A sign that you should pledge allegiance, swallow a handful of
Easter eggs and sidewalk chalk
And feel it feel so good,
warming the neon passageways to your heart
And feel it feel like home.

Yoyo

My heart will double as a yoyo
in the event of your boredom.

Strange Pleasures Part 1

Cassidy was a strange girl—she loved getting sun burnt.
Her skin thinned and became clear as new ice;
where she pressed, tiny white flower shapes bloomed.
Lying in the sand she'd fall asleep,
wake up with an ultraviolet sting.
At night the fever came.
Her bones themselves shivered.
Hard to explain the pleasure:
Transcendent.

Praying for Syria

I was supposed to be praying for Syria
and atoning for my sins
but when I looked down at my stomach protruding behind
white lace
like a plump and greedy bride, I felt the units of serotonin
sucked up out of
wherever the fuck they're supposed to be
and a steel wool veil dropped down behind my chest and melted
to thick, ductile plasma and I thought I'd rather evaporate into
thin air
than stand with the construct of God, God the character
while he whispered in my ear
that I would never be good enough

and the rabbi said over and over again
how God gave us purely good souls—
no matter what you've done, your soul is purely good
and you should never feel shame—but God snuck back down
to remind me that this applies only to everyone else,
and that yes,
in fact,
I should feel shame,
because of remember that thing that happened
in the interim between me creating your soul and me slipping
it into your body like a letter into an envelope?
Don't you remember your airy intangible being getting snagged
on a sycamore where mockingbirds hung from tiny nooses
and swayed

ever so lightly in the hot breeze?
But no, I don't remember
I just feel it built into my cells: my soul feeds it to them daily
trying to shake itself of the ashy residue.

So I had to put my face in my hands
to keep it from running off
Dalí style
and my sister leaned in to say Mom Wants to Know if
You're Okay?
And I hissed "I'm praying for Syria" though by then I had
long since moved on
to the poem forming in the empty gaps between my
scattered serotonin
and the thought that maybe my soul lives in between my legs
and is heavy with mockingbirds decomposing
and the wet velvet of guilty-pleasured, perverted nostalgia,
the wet velvet of agitated, impatient appetite
and I will be eternally burdened by an Original Sin that
wasn't even mine.

The congregation read aloud: "Dear Lord, we live to serve you"
and more than anything in the world I wanted to be back
in your Downtown loft with red walls
and tiled floors
and the screen that loomed over us while you projected
Italian horror films
and your warped subconscious onto them
in Technicolor. I wanted to be drunk on Jameson and Ativan
and your Tom Ford Noir de Noir For Men
like the night you smashed a vase and I cleaned up the pieces

covered in your blood, "Loving You Sometimes" by the Outsiders
on repeat,
or the night you put American Psycho up
on the big screen
and dressed me up in thigh-highs, made me crawl
across the floor to you, half man half wolf and I--
I was half girl half wind-up doll,
and it was all so deliciously unfair
and imbalanced like a highly unlikely accident you never knew
God Himself was planning all along.

So I looked around and wondered
of all these bowed and cloth-capped heads
how many believe in God?
And out of those, how many believe He gives a fuck?
And how many of those recognize his sadism
how many of those recognize he's a daddy dom with a Tumblr blog
who had to punish the ship that thought it couldn't sink
in a hissy fit when for a second it seemed He had lost control
of the game?

Sometimes I'm scrolling through Tumblr porn and think *Fuck,*
I've been to that house
with the imitation Rothkos and a view
of the wrong side of Mulholland.
And sometimes I go to La Scala
for chopped salads
just to make up for the fact that I missed the Golden Age of
Chasens,
missed the Less Than Zero era
by a day.

Watch the Rain

I wrote a poem in my dream last night, it went like this:
Take drugs/be photographed/sit on a hotel bed/watch
the rain.

Photographs From a Disposable Camera

I

The moon, tonight, is sterling silver;
raw, too-polished
multidimensional glass figurine I would break
had it a place on my shelf
(among the cat and the rabbit whose pieces shattered into
shattered pieces of myself).

The moon is tangled up in ink and tree branches;
wiry, possessive.
The trees are not entirely in silhouette, leaves glow amber and emerald like
Disney lanterns, moth wings flickering in the wind, backlit by the moon and
smaller spheres from across the street,
fixed onto walls/turned on for nobody.

An icy current generates itself through the sky,
colors that burn with the harp-like tone of twilight.
The sky is periwinkle on the end of the spectrum where the color thins to blue;
silken, diaphanous / woven entirely from gossamer / threads pulled tightly together / meticulous web stretched to the far edges of sanity.

The woven fabric is fleshy and delicate like an inner layer
of skin laced through with a network of electric veins.

If we used our teeth against it, there would be blood.
It is blue blood, we see, flowing and clotting behind that
intangible flesh.
The sky is made from energy and plasma,
web of our collective dreaming.

I inhale smoke from a Camel Light that does not feel like
mine and will never.
When I cough, I sound like my mother.
We are sitting, you and I, on a grass covered slope just above
the Greek Theatre,
two or three thousand people filling in the concrete spaces
beneath us.
They are the colors in our drawing book, filling empty space
within lines of our design.
There are much more of them than I imagined You say.
I had not imagined them at all.

By the time it is dark
we are damp with mist and high expectations.
My hands smell like yours do: tobacco, arrogance.
San Francisco Lights are visible in the distance.

The patchwork of moonlight and shadow
turns the grass to velvet beneath us.
I lean into you / we into it /
your legs on either side of me / your arms around my neck /
you say *I'll catch you.*

I think I'll love you for trying.

My blacks become your blues.
We are all denim and cotton and leather,
stripes and plaids and bruises.

You kiss my fingertips and
I have wanted to feel this way: a child, again
hoping the mist will become rain / preferring the cold and
the grey /
feeling safest in October.

II

Jane-Marie is waiting at the station
        like she said she would
                at three o'clock—

Sitting quiet and her legs crossed—
        as I step towards her
                she wipes the mascara bleeding from her
eyes.

This is not ugly
    as it is

                crippled

Not beautiful
    as it is
    obscure

                and seamless. We string thread
                    through needles and watch
disappear

all that we have sewn.

That day
her skin bleached
    and dry
        and grey
her golden hair in struggled knots
still caught
    and reflected
    all light from the sun

and she was still looking
    like a dream of winter
        spun from light and dust

Even in the station
    even on the main street

        of a stranger city she does not love.

This is why
    we censor lovers
    this is why
        we dislike nature
    this is why we wish for Halloween
        and Greyhound
        and Southwest
        and the Twelfth of December.

But at least,
    they say,

        you have TV and Cafés and
                Bookstore Consolations.
And at least
    they say,
        you have Gourmet Ice Cream and Clothing
and
                Public
Transportation.

III

Dawn introduces a new song.
It is the break between melodies
golden where chords wait for each other: the darkest
parts of midnight meet the dusty rush of morning.
And that is dawn, the sound in between which envelopes my
mind. And my mind to yours.
And your hands to mine, forcing us to be strangers no more.
And that is dawn, the binding commandment
that forces strangeness away
and begs for attention
without saying anything on the subject, so you do not know it
is begging your attention
but you give it anyway
because it has been hours since sun
and you think perhaps there are answers to the night's
questions in this new fabric
of light and fluidity that ripples in the wind
swelling slowly up from the horizon
then spilling, suddenly, proclaiming itself a new day and
admitting to having no answers

but by then you've found resolution in other songs and
deliberate dancing
and it is enough to watch the moonlight lines
(which once had filtered in through window blinds)
disappear into the past.
And it is enough to have a hand to hold,
a heart that knows the story of the nightingale who
drained her blood
for the love of somebody who did not notice
because that was all you wanted:
somebody who knew the same story
and would read it out loud
to soften the brutality of morning.

Do you think about falling asleep together
and premature midnight
and frozen film strips forcing away the day
and landing among Technicolor like
collective dreaming
like splintered prayers?
You say
There Is Nothing More Beautiful
than A City In The Distance.
You say
Most Of Humanity Did Not Get A Chance To See The
World This Way:
Frightened and Small and Explosive and Unaware.
And broken. And
Fake and
Too real.

You say
Black Coffee
and Bubbles
and
We Have Never Been In Water
Together, Before
And I wonder if that means we are clean now,
now that we turn our thoughts into bubbles and
send them to each other
or write them on glass.
And you say
We're Sinking and
Let's Pretend That We Are Dead. And you say
We're Sinking
When really you mean The Water Is Draining
And I say
Are We Sinking? And you say
No, We're Rising.
The Ferris Wheel flashes color across your face
like truth, like death
like being reborn every two seconds
in red, in yellow, in white
in blue, in green, in perforated light
and you say
Can You See It From San Francisco?
and I say
Yes
though I've been trying not to lie,
I promise
and I say

Yes
even though I am afraid
and I am smoky and bruised
and often on fire and I
Am Tired
and cannot listen to *Wild World* by Cat Stevens
Without crying
and you say
You're Still Here
And I say
No, It Only Looks That Way, I Am Really Split Between
Oblivions
With A Bubble Wrap Heart
Written On With Permanent Marker
And you say
Pop. Pop pop pop pop pop
and your mouth is like
A neon exit sign
and I say
My Fingertips Are Bleeding
And every part of me that knows how to bleed
is bleeding
and I say
I Must Be Dying
and you say
Since When Do You Wear Makeup?
and I say
I'm Not
and you say
Not What?

and I say
Wearing Makeup
and you say
But There Is A Dark Color Around Your Eyes.
And I say
That Isn't Makeup, It Is A String Of Sentences Made From Yesterday's Wishes.
And you say
But Your Mouth is Red
And I say
You Made It That Way.
Then one day, when we have enough time to do so
and be worriless,
I will ask you when you first decided to love me
And what you are thinking each time you say it.
You will explain,
because you have nothing but time to do so;
Your words drawing lines through a map of Forever
leading us,
eventually,
back home.

Another Fucking Taylor Swift Poem

It was 2010 and I asked my boyfriend at the time
what he thought accounted for Taylor Swift's epic success.
What I meant was: what has made her stand out against
all the other blonde pop stars
that seem to fade so fast
you get whiplash
trying to keep track?
He said
she's making country youthful again
—remember, this was 2010—
but that's not really the point.
The point is that this was a decade ago, this was just
the beginning for Taylor
but I already knew she was here to stay.
And that terrifies me.

Nobody Lives Here

5:00 AM in the house off Mulholland
with an elitist view of a city bellow
seemingly abandoned, hollowed
out, gutted, a million eyes
glittering up out of the empty, wondering.

Where the master bed is suspended by ropes
that disappear into a ceiling some fifty feet above.
Where the girls are topless and tan
makeup dripping,
lounging loosely into anyone with arms.
Where nobody has bothered to arrange
the cocaine
into lines, little indecipherable words
of wisdom or warning.

Nobody knows who owns the house—
Somebody is renting it from somebody
who is renting it from somebody who is in
Investment Banking or
Drug Dealing or
Doesn't Exist.
Naked bodies drop from a brick wall
into the blackest pool.
"Somebody is going to die eventually" I say as a girl goes head-
first
into the rippling black and spectators comment

using Olympic speak:
I give it an 8.5, very little splash but not enough form.
"Babe, everybody is going to die eventually" somebody retorts, delayed
and there is laughter
as if this is very clever.

Don't Be Cruel by Elvis
plays from hidden speakers in every room and in the trees.
I have always felt so disconnected from Elvis.
Now, especially
now that I can't determine where his voice is coming from
but it is everywhere, background music for the following visual:
naked bodies rise
slowly from the water
one by one, dry their hands and check for text messages, emails, tweets, then
make their way back to the pool. #Autopilot.
As I—in hot water—
look up into the faces of pristine constellations adhering to the sky
from which the pool water derives its black.
So easy to forget the constellations.
So easy to pretend they aren't there.

Alice has fake tits and wants me to touch them.
She says, "I always felt like a girl with big tits
trapped inside a flat girl's body."
I tell her I have always felt the opposite.

"I'm scared one day they will start leaking
from the inside"
she confides,
"and silicone will poison my blood stream."
"Is it worth it?" I ask.
"I wish I hadn't been born," she says.

Oxy-codeine moon-light of a window-rippled street-lamp

The first of two-dozen gold balloons
sinks to the floor at twelve o' clock the morning after

and, echoing from the open door,
the ghosts of self-negligent children and their drunken laughter

dancing around the floor of a champagne-wet new year
in a room
that is only the memory of a wooden gazebo in the rain.
They write their names into the foggy glass, trying only to
see clear: *Alice in Wonderland, Wizard of Oz,*
and What Ever Happened to Baby Jane?

The first one to be smashed said *don't worry*
she said
I'm not a glass of orange juice--I won't spill
I said,
That's good, but
this one thought is too big for my entire body, so
tonight I definitely will

when Los Angeles overdoses on some numbing pill
and a glimpse of cold generates through the city
and, though concerned, the children are thrilled
and the dark settles in, but the darkness is pretty.

It makes me think of falling in love, but nothing yet very certain
as the oxy-codeine moon-light of a window-rippled street-lamp
gushes in through green-winter curtains:

your anesthetic left me with the yearn for certain burns and
an infatuation with every moment's bleeding screen.

Dislocation 1

All these brunette heroines
sublunary skin   eyes   like holes in time.
          Falling into her   is falling
into   darkness
that everybody wants   because
              it frightens.

Everybody wants   to lie beneath
warm   damp   shadow.

Ella imagines that running   her fingers
along the   dilated stacks of desert
        would feel like   his petal-soft skin
she could not   sink   beneath.

It didn't seem   fair: the desert
had grown   itself inside her.

Dislocation 2

Strawberry and   cold water blow like

smoke over   tiny iron   bones

and   that   is

her: medicine

for   red lamé trauma   victims, you will feel so

good

tonight

really   really   good,

too good.

We'll live on   empty
rooftops of   stimulant necessity   where

virgin   hearts are pulled apart to
tenuous
web-like
strings over time,
writingopaquesymphoniesacrosstheceilinginlinesofquietlight.

Ignore the girls   dancing naked   on   poles,
though they've written their story   lines

into your arms
and you will never be able to look
away.

Put this powder under your tongue and breathe.
Put your jack deep inside my box to hear the music, if you
know what I mean.

Midnight and Always

I think about you at midnight.
And also always.

Misha

First, you were a Xeroxed, photocopied image
vague, pixilated
dream-colored figurine printed from the Internet
something new, then.

You were a seed planted, a milestone tossed
at the base of the new millennium
that someday you would come to own
sitting on your velvet, antique thrown
as though you knew you would be king.

You were happiest at Trout Lake
submerged beneath the glassy surface, reflecting cobalt.
We got high off of air too thin to breathe
strolling the boardwalks of a monopolized town
where purple money and silver thimbles
made and followed rules.
Our laughter dry with a lack of oxygen
broke and departed into the lonely room.

You killed fish and dropped them at my feet.
I captured you on film, wondering what you dreamt
about (If anything
at all)
wondering if you knew that you would die—
sometimes the way you stared off, burdened and concerned
it seemed as though you did.

As far as home movies go, I have you captured
in eternity's sullen stare
but your memory is like a snowflake
pristine, evanescent;
You melt in my palm
leaving a cold, silver trail.

What were you like?
It is difficult to recall
when your happy replica is asleep in my arms:
her jagged teeth like pieces broken from the moon
leave violent lines across my skin
as yours once did.
Now you are a radiant shadow, silent luminosity
that comes to me at night—
you are everywhere and anywhere that there is light.

I still want to know what you dream about.
I want to know if you are dreaming, still.

Thoughts in Vermont

Thought: if only one part of my body is to get into heaven, which will it be?
Then thought: I know which it will not be.

The Drive Home from Moonshadows

Holes blink golden from the nighttime's navy skin
some small, inflicted by shards of glass
others full and swollen where something more serious has occurred.
I cannot help but think of you,
the way you smile at any type of wound
and tell me there's nothing to be concerned about.

The sky has died, and will continue to die
more times than even the cat.
Her ten million funerals makes nine a failure
falling each night from her pale blue pedestal
idiotically cheerful
and stitched with the sun's conciliatory threads.

Her smile fades gracefully, her knees buckle in relief
the light goes out in a pleasured farewell sigh--
she dies exceptionally well, I can't die at all.

And tonight she makes a spectacle of it:
splintered light of acidic color flooding from her eyes
settling among the graveyard of our pacific roadway
littered with painted metal and drowned in the red and white
glow of independence and traffic light

where we've rushed idly towards darkness
like bodies down hospital hallways

on plastic beds with wheels because of some accident
idly towards the wounds which stubbornly evade us
ashamed and insane with truths:

regrets and a lie,
perhaps a warning, perhaps a confession--
perhaps they are in love with us,
or some other horror they will not say.
Lonely constellations, they've tired themselves out.

From you, now, I am full of these holes:
my skin chewed through, second-rate as moth ridden satin
my chocolate heart invaded by your maggots,

I am the leftovers from your masterpiece.

X-BOX (conversations with a four-year-old)
For Scarlett

Why are you being
like this?

I don't know
       I juh
       don't
       know.

You've been

screaming   for half an hour.

I'm not
I'm not mad
I'm
juh jad becau
dey were mad
at me.

Because you weren't cleaning.
It was everyone's responsibility to clean—

And alcho and
alcho um…
and alcho I'm chyin' becau you
took away
eh-boh   *fwom me.*

I took away x box
because you weren't cleaning.　　　　　It was
everyone's responsibility
and you
were not working.

Do Kewen and Autumn get it?

Kellen definitely. He was working.

How about Autumn,　　　do she?

………Do she?

I don't know. I have to find out if—

She wah pwayin' den she was cheanin'.

Will you　　　　please　　　　stop crying?

I juh can't…I juh can't top chying becau Kewen and
*　　Autumn are still mad at me and*
*　　　　I juh*
*　　　　　　cant*
*　　　　　　　　top*
*　　　　　　　　　　becau*
Im aw awooooonnne!!!!!!!!!!!!!!!!!!!!!!!!!!!!!!!!

You're not all					alone

baby. I'm right here

with you.
We
all
love
you
very
much.

Iwuvyoutoo.

Hint

Ask me if I care. (Hint: I do).

Red Vines

The air is thinner up here
I think, ringing your doorbell, then wonder how I've ended up
exactly where I knew I'd end up today.

I've driven to dizzying heights just to counteract the notion
that I am nobody—
a notion that flickers and falters with my finger pressed against
the bell
and my reflection trapped inside your door
mapped out in no more
than three or four shades of gray.

Eating Red Vines on an empty stomach with
a view of just about everything
sprawled out below,
I'm taken back to a time when I inhaled licorice
in vapor form [they called this flavor *Rotten Rope*]
all day and held it in my lungs like an antiseptic, until one night
I woke to the very end of Hunger Games [Mocking Jay, Part One]
and credits rolled
and Lorde sang *Yellow Flicker Beat*
and there was a pain in my throat so fiery and so sordid
I thought surely this is the tongue of hell rising up
to claim me.

Through the candied fog of all this you explain yourself to me
the best you can

while I chew my licorice,
and Lorde help me because
the way you make me feel is liquor-ish—
wet and quenched to my core—
and as it turns out I can get high off self-deprivation
just as I can get high off indulgence in
all my favorite lies shattered and glittering, embedded deep
in the bricks
in the walls
of the underworld wonderland
I still dream of falling into.

Strange Pleasures Part 2

Cassidy flossed her teeth nightly just like you're supposed to.

She dug the minty wax string into her gums.

Blood surfaced like tiny rubies in liquid form.

The pain was sharp and deep, profound.

Her heartbeat in between teeth.

She watched TV before bed.

She savored the pain.

Waves of pain.

Crashing like:

aaaaaaaaaa

aaaaaa

aaagg

gggg

ggg

gg

g

h

h

h.

What You Did

I return home smelling of new york city--
I am cramped and guilty,
complaining that he won't wash away
complaining of the misery which clots the breeze
and stream of sun which flooded from the north.
I taste it, sweet as deflation, in gift chocolates and teas

sweet as the most chemical of roses--
corroded, their petals only rust and blister
in a new room
where the light of stars and wings of moths just flicker:
their passions extinguished by the disease
of an insipid lullaby.

I've stopped hearing from you on most days
and so we've hardly any time to count the tragedies
that collected so nicely--
salt crystals on your lips
bricks in the walls of my cellar:
Blue stone, safe haven.

That is, you left me alone in this wooden town
infected by rainbow sprinkles and ballerina clowns.
No umbilical constrictions, no red, nightly medications
what type of asylum is this?
Asylum which taunts me with the foreign hymns of
wedding bells

and the elated drone
of the innocent skipping stones
in a brook just beyond the borders of my windowsill.

I've chased you through the static streets
through filth, the sin, and faltering, electronic heart beats--
each patent leather step, a fallen note
in the pavement's crippled song
each blood-stained breath, a note in the siren's strident call
only so I could see your pretty eyelashes and say
"You have not changed at all, you have not changed at all."

On Coney Island, I insisted the ocean remain a platonic love
afraid such waters would take you from me.
I watched the girls with stripes and cigarettes be cleansed
as I cut open the healing blisters of curiosity
(the healing blisters of consequential agony).

What an awful excuse: the stars have told me what to do
the stars which tear themselves from the sky,
only so we could lie together to watch them fall
and you could see my pretty eyelashes and say
"You have not changed at all, you have not changed at all."

Very Rich

"You are very young," he said, "and I am very rich."

You Said You Would

Girls who draw you drawings
and send them in the mail.
Girls who write you songs and sing them
wildly, so rampantly self-unaware.

Girls who know their bodies are gifts
and lay them across your bed.

Girls who never would have looked twice
get snagged on your hooks
so easily.

And it's hard to believe
Hard to understand.

I don't believe it
And I don't understand it,

even though I am that girl, and in my own mind
I am the queen of them all.
With your hook buried deep, I am the most snagged of the snagged
hanging like an ornament
still dreaming that you'll untangle me from that gnarled
metal thistle, pluck me from where I'm connected
at my waist flesh
and fly me first-class to another galaxy entirely

where we'll read books on white-sand beaches
and listen to music from crickets the color of peaches
and you'll look out the window at me in my blue Lycra bikini
with my mouth wrapped around a red lollipop
just like you said you would.

In Case You're Wondering

The price of my love is one post-it note with a parenthesis written on it. Like this: ( )
(Just remember that love comes and goes —and that whoever promises their love will last forever doesn't have the authority to make such a promise).

Carpe Noctum

I've been telling myself that a guy like you
doesn't deserve a poem by a girl like me
because wanting you means squandering all that I am
when to you
girls like me
are a dime a dozen.

But like a tick you're deep in the tissue of my brain
and you'll stay there forever if I don't make this cut
to let you out.

And I'd be lying if I said I never saw you coming.
Would you believe me if I said
a babysitter once read my palm and predicted you, the
wrench, opening up my life?
I was seven then and didn't like the thought of you
in a white t-shirt in the lobby of a doorman building on
the Upper East Side.
She told me you had money and came with a warning.
So, fifteen years later when
I was drinking apple martinis in a broken-mirrored room
on the corner of Hollywood Boulevard and saw you
standing in the accidental spotlight of a purposefully
crooked fixture
I was only half surprised.

It was the 9th of January and I had resolutions to roll like a rolling stone.
They dared me to talk to you and I thought
carpe noctum.

Strange Pleasures Part 3

You hear about girls who cut themselves with razor blades. Cassidy wasn't one of them—she didn't want scars. Instead, she used heavy objects to make bruises.
The remote control hard against her shin.
Repeatedly, she hit until vessels broke.
The skin became puffy, red.
Yellow, blue, purple, black.
That endorphin soreness.
Those colors.
Ecstatic.

Degrees of Sparkle

I woke up in New York City
remembering but not remembering
ordering coffee and a donut at JFK
pouring ice water into the coffee
when it was already too late—
a bubble of burnt skin already forming on my hand,
followed by an angry red line
like a tadpole.

I needed somewhere air-conditioned to lay my head,
but the best I could do was sit in a hotel lobby somewhere
in the west village
watching travelers and business people file in
following easy paths to their rooms
and it was torture.

I wished you were there with me.
but not just you.
I wished you'd bring a five-star hotel room like a shell on
your back
and you'd set it up for me like you've set yourself up in my mind
and we'd wear bathrobes
drinking elderflower and adrenaline
from each other's cupped hands.

Without liquor
my bones have nothing to float on and

light leaks out from a hole in me
continuously.
I want to be filled up with you
to keep the light inside
and we'll tumble together like fiber optic weeds
into a void of additive color.

When I was ten I stopped living in the right body, my real body.
My real body is flat chested without hips
with a pussy folded neatly into itself, modest and
unconcerned with its purpose.
My real body is an introvert
ambushed by inevitably pornographic breasts
and a pussy in full bloom
petals reaching hungrily
like the split and splayed shotgun shells
I used to pluck from desert dust.

I can't have my real body back
so I eat numbers.
Numbers are safe to eat.

New York is a hilarious cliché of itself:

A man reading Fountainhead while waiting for the F train
that screeches to a halt like the devil's fingernails
scratching against a chalkboard.
It is too hot and there's a rat on the tracks,
fat with mischief.

People are waiting around and then rushing
then waiting around again.
Among the rushers, people taking their time seem absurd,
even obscene
drunk with the ultimate luxury of time.
There is a girl in all black holding a metrocard in her teeth,
nostalgic for tokens and
the taste of metal
and I am a girl in a dress with a notebook
eager to flee the scene.

I walk around New York like I don't deserve to be in New York,
like I'm going to get in trouble
for being in New York.
Like the New York City Worthiness Committee
is taking notes, writing citations.
They're going to descend on me
like bats
as I walk down west twenty-second street.

Does the man selling bottled water in the park
for four dollars
feel bad about charging four dollars,
or does he think it's fair?
Will my boyfriend's daughter one day realize that
I sometimes mistake her for me
and become fixated on shielding myself via her, from the world?
A second chance at innocence maintained.

On benzodiazepines I realized that the
prickly hairs on my body are protection
and in that way, I am like a cactus.
I realized that sex is actually
the perpetual stabbing of a never-healing wound
and that trying to figure out why something turns you on
is like trying to explain why a joke is funny:
it snuffs every degree of sparkle right out.

Sorry

In a dream there was a polar bear man with a penguin on a leash, and a girl I thought hated me put her arms around my neck because she knew the penguin was dangerous. She had tattoos of purple flowers on her wrists and I kept trying to say sorry for all the things I had said behind her back.

Madison Avenue

I saw a mannequin lounging in a decked-out window
on Madison Avenue
rhinestones adhered to her white, white skin
and I was jealous of her because
of her wall-flat stomach and jutting hipbones
and because she didn't have to be real.

On the corner I overheard two homeless men
say that most of their dollar bills come from kids.
Kids are the generous ones, one said,
so I gave him fifteen dollars hoping maybe I could go back.

When I was a kid, I spent almost all my time
wondering what I'd be like as an adult.
I never thought in a million years
I'd spend almost all of my life remembering
what I was like as a child
and wanting to go back.

You sunk stakes into my brain
Set up camp in that gray terrain.
You talk of a theoretical girl
who is empty-headed in a charming way.
I'll hunt her down tear her limb from limb.

Selfish

I'm sitting in a chapel
In a college in Vermont
With a pipe organ that looks
Like a pack of cigarettes to everyone
Except to me. To me it looks like a set
Of plastic nail extensions
Waiting to be clipped and filed into shape.

I'm sitting in this chapel
Listening to a visiting poet
Read about guns that give their victims orgasms
Instead of death
When I think about you, and how I wish you were here.
More specifically, how I wish you could sit behind me
And knead my shoulders with your two fingers,
The way you like to do,
Run them over the misaligned pearls of my spine
Organizing them one by one until they are a necklace
Until I am not broken, not undone
anymore.

When we are at home in our two-bedroom nest
In a development in Playa Vista
With two pools and the central air conditioning
I've always dreamed of
I think this is the safest place on earth.
You lie face down on the carpet and I walk on your back

A balancing act with the TV on
Connecting my bare feet to your skin and muscle and bone,
Sinking my roots into you and hoping they grow.
I never wanted to live
In a place that had carpet
But I don't think we'd be able
To do this
Without it.

And is it selfish
If I wish
Sometimes
That our roles could be reversed?
That I could lie face down on the carpet
And you could walk on me
Crushing out the knots and the kinks
Wringing out the venom and toxins that writhe around my thoughts
Until all I have are thoughts of you
And the feeling of your footprints?
But more true than that is this:
I wish I knew you
Half as well as you know me.
In your hands I am a frog princess.
You cut me open, dissected me and read my insides
Like a map
Of a world
You call ZZ.
Then you sewed me up
And since then it's like you've had me memorized.

That's a skill
And a talent.

Each year you buy a birthday present that corresponds
With the various color-coded fragments of my heart
And I don't understand: are your standards low
or am I as amazing
As you say I am?

This year you
And your children
Gave me videos of you
And your children
From the gap in time before I knew you
From the gap in time before I knew your children.
What I hate is that you knew
That this is what I wanted most
That this is what would make me happy
And so you made it happen
And so I'm watching these videos alone
And what I don't think you realized is that I'd see
In between the precious moments
How suddenly you were excommunicated
without being excommunicated
From the people you made
And how much they wanted you back.
It makes me want to cut open the past
And re-arrange its brittle pieces
Then sew it all back together so that life was still your life
And your children were little flowers blooming
In your hands
Forever.

But if I did that then
You wouldn't have met me,
So I won't do that.
And is that selfish?

This year you paid good money
To have my identity shipped across the country.
You added in a pair of pants and a tin of cookies
With a piece of bread on top.
Everyone knew that the piece of bread was there to keep the Cookies moist
Except me.

The best and only good part
About being away from you
Is that I can fall asleep watching pretty little liars
And not feel bad about it.

First Love

You know when you have a key that fits in the lock, but isn't the right one to make it turn? It's like that.

Pen to Paper

I put pen to paper
but it doesn't make it any better
it doesn't make it any easier
to keep my eyes open. They're nothing but mousetraps
ready to snap.

So snap, I beg, just let me sleep
let me never wake up from this fever dream
let me shut my eyes for the final time
but God, never let me die.

A moment unconscious is a moment I'm free, a moment
I treasure
yet the thought of death fucks me up, brings me no pleasure.
Thinking of my existence vanished from the planet
chills my bones so cold they feel hot
screaming at me to fight against inevitable demise
screaming at me so swim against the tides
please don't let me vanish
and yet…

Are songwriters better than people who can't write songs?
Does God love them more?
It's hard to look at Taylor Swift's real estate portfolio
count the square footage
and not worry God loves her more.

It's hard to look at someone who has fun
spinning pain into platinum
and not think God loves her more.

I have no choice but to put pen to paper.
It doesn't make it any better, doesn't make me special.
It doesn't turn the pain
into any precious gem or metal.
I still miss my home
and it feels like a knife in my spleen
I still miss ordering imaginative cocktails
even more than I miss drinking.

This is not the time to think about everything I'm not
or the defects I can't tame.
The world is on fire, but my ego thrives in flame
spreading through me like a virus
crawling through my blood like spiders:
You will feel ashamed.

Let's keep going, we are mining.
We? I am mining.
I am deep in a shaft of fool's gold and I'll take it.
I am the fool after all
believing my own lies
believing in pop star poetry and brain medicine
believing, sometimes, that my visions shape constellations
that my visions pluck stars from the sky.
I wear them on my fingers and in my ears,
I wear them around my neck:

light caught in a diamond looks like fireflies
struggling in a web
struggling like a girl drowning in praise.
Maybe next time she'll be careful what she wishes for.
Or maybe the high wears off in days
and is gone like a memory shoved in a bottle washed ashore.

I put pen to paper, but it didn't make it any better.
I put stories in my head, and they knit themselves sweaters.
Set up shop forever.

Maybe there are already enough song writers.
Maybe the world doesn't need one more.

Diet Coke

Does anybody want this bottle
of Diet Coke?

I bought it by accident.
I wanted a regular Coke, actually.

But there is absolutely nothing wrong
with this bottle of Diet Coke. It has a silvery label
decorated simply with a snowflake
and a polar bear,
and I'm sure I'd drink it
if I hadn't been raised not to touch the stuff,
the neurotoxins and the sugar stand-ins.

If at night you pulled out a tooth
and put it in a bottle of Diet Coke
by morning the tooth would be dissolved,
they say.

But you won't be pulling out any teeth
and leaving them in this bottle over night
so you should be fine,
you will survive
this bottle of Diet Coke.

I didn't think I was the kind of girl
to write a poem about Diet Coke
but there, I did it.

Strange Pleasures Part 4

Then there was that other thing she loved to do.

She went to rock concerts, sang her heart out.

When she forgot the words, she just screamed.

She'd wake up the next day, voiceless.

As if it had been stolen.

By an evil sea witch.

She couldn't answer questions.

She mouthed replies:

Leave me.

Alone.

Apocalypse Currently

Too much shame to unravel
blue sea glass in gravel,
I start to think in stanzas
whenever it rains.

Only safe in pajamas
my new pathology:
Honey Bunches of Oats,
the best plan to kill me slow.

I walk for hours
wondering if my life is really my own.
The houses in West Hollywood with yards and gates and
big tv glow…
I am an adult now, so

The Bestsellers

Studies show that people want to read
about human closeness. Shared bonds. Intimacy.
They want to read about
marriage, death, taxes and
technologies, kids, doctors, moms, media,
work, school, presidents, newspapers, funerals
and guns.
They want to read about the average home.
They want to read about the stock market, laboratories,
spirituality, and college.
They want to read about dogs.

Studies show that people do not want to read
about seduction,
cigarettes, alcohol, or
revolutions.
They do not want to read
about sojourns, dinner parties, playing cards,
or very dressed up
women.
They do not want to read about the Gods.
They do not want to read about wheeling and dealing, graphic
sex, drugs, or rock n' roll.
They do not want to read about worship,
or witches.
They do not want to read about the human body
unless it is at a crime scene.

Studies show that
Bestselling characters express their needs.
Wants are good too, but needs are even better.
Bestselling characters
grab, do, think, ask, look, hold, love, tell, like, see, hear, smile,
reach, pull, push, start, work, know, arrive, spend, walk, pray,
hug, talk, read, imagine, decide, believe, love, hate, see, stare,
scream, shove, miss, eat, nod, open, close, say, sleep,
type, watch, turn,
run, shoot,
kiss,
die.

Studies show that characters
who don't sell,
tend to shout, fling, whirl, thrust,
murmur, protest,
hesitate,
accept,
dislike, seem,   suppose,
recover. They tend to grunt,
clutch,   peer,   gulp, tremble, cling,
jerk, shiver, break, fumble,   fling.
They tend to begin, accept,   remark, exclaim,
mutter,   answer,
protest, address,
shout,   demand,
and

speak.

Toxic

People will do anything
say anything
to prove that their love
their lifestyle
isn't toxic.

Your boyfriend is fifty and pays your rent
you do coke for dinner and stay up 'til dawn.
He doesn't mind
when you're with other guys
in fact he likes it
wants to hear about it.
He sleeps with more women
than you knew existed.
Oh, and he has a kid;
She's around your age and you actually get along really well.

And yes I'm judging you.
I'm not saying you're bad or wrong
I'm saying this isn't healthy.
I'm saying you just have no idea
the nutrients you're missing out on when you plant yourself
in artificial soil.
I'm saying you're impressed by Styrofoam snow
because you've spent your whole life in LA
and I would know
because I'm not all that different from you.

I was raised in the land of mixed messages
and plastic standards
and sometimes my compass spins out of control
and I think down is up
and I take my clothes off under false pretense.
I've been down this road.
It's the wrong direction on a one-way street
in Downtown LA
with "Ride" by Lana Del Rey
playing on repeat. It's the art of screaming and crying and
punching the steering wheel until you're numb.
I guess I'm just jealous
of anyone
who has succeeded
at being numb.

Some of you have no idea what I'm talking about.
Some of you do.

Walking Home Alone in a Pandemic

The first night I walked home alone
in a pandemic
it didn't occur to me
that it would be any different from the other nights
walking home alone
with my dog at my side and my wits about me.

But it was midnight between Friday and Saturday
and there was absolutely nobody
on the streets. No cars on the road. No noise to be heard
except for the orchestra of crickets
the water fountains in front lawns
gurgling and hidden.
I listened for the sound of telephone wires
whispering clues like soda poured over ice
but even they didn't know what the fuck was going on.

A silent city. A shut-in city. A city locked down.
I walked from Romaine onto Crescent Heights thinking
never before in History
have the streets of Los Angeles known such stillness.
Suburbia-grade stillness. Rural-grade stillness. Santa
Monica Boulevard with its lights out. Jay-walking because
I could. Because it was easy. Because it would have been
stupid not to. A world put on hold, suspended in time
kind of
like I'd always wanted.

The streets were dead, but the air was alive with electrons and smelled clean
not like the calm before the storm, but the calm right after
and I made myself promise I'd remember it forever.

But we get into trouble
when we think time belongs to us, when we think we can hold on.
I miss every moment as soon as it's gone.

I Could Sleep Forever

I could sleep forever
and sometimes I think I should.
This guy on twitter I don't even know wrote
Writers, one of these has to go : ; ...
and it sent me into an inexplicable rage.
It's not that I'm some punctuation maniac
in fact I'm not
and often like to throw it out the window entirely
just for fun and because I can

So why did I get so mad? I think because
how dare he tell writers: what to do;
How dare he fuck with—the tools—we use to build walls…

Baby, I am so tired.
I've only been back on my words bullshit
for two weeks now
and already I am so tired of it. Once you realize
Everything is poetry, you're fucked. Or: you're…free…?

The words catapult like
cannonballs and I can not catch them all.
To be tired and under fire when
the world is on the perpetual brink of revolution
is to feel completely worthless.
And damn,
I'm already prone to overlooking my worth.

Zara Lisbon is the author of *Fake Plastic Girl* and *Fake Plastic World*. *Baby's First Apocalypse* is her first book of poetry.

www.ingramcontent.com/pod-product-compliance
Lightning Source LLC
Chambersburg PA
CBHW022013120526
44592CB00034B/800